LONGMAN ORIGINALS Stage
Series editor: Robert C

MW01708774

The Forger

Robert O'Neill

Illustrations by Mike Bambury

Longman

Longman Group UK Limited,
Longman House, Burnt Mill, Harlow,
Essex CM20 2JE, England
and Associated Companies throughout the world

First published 1974 in Longman Structural Readers
This edition first published 1992 in Longman Originals
Third impression 1994

Set in 11/13pt Melior, Adobe/Linotype (postscript)

Produced by Longman Singapore Publishers Pte Ltd
Printed in Singapore

ISBN 0 582 07494 0

Contents

CHAPTER ONE

The burglar

The burglar looked down from the roof. The lights of Paris were below. The Eiffel Tower was in the distance. It shone brightly in the night. The view was beautiful. But the burglar hadn't come to enjoy the view. There was work to be done.

It was just past midnight. A few drops of rain were falling and the roof was wet and dangerous. It was the roof of a small art gallery. The gallery sold paintings to rich people all over the world. Some of the paintings inside were worth very large amounts of money.

The burglar had very clear orders. The day before, in another city, an old man had said, "Don't break any windows. Leave no sign that you've been in the gallery. Take the painting and then get out. Nobody must know what has happened. Do exactly what I've told you!"

It wasn't easy. Only an expert could do it. But the burglar was an expert. An expert with a cool, clear head, strong hands and the body of a trained athlete. The burglar knew everything about the gallery. There were burglar alarms all over the gallery, of course. If anybody tried to get in at night, the alarms would ring. The police would be there in a few minutes. But there was one window that didn't have an alarm. It was very small and it was just below the roof. It didn't seem possible that anyone could get through it from the outside. That was why there was no alarm there.

The burglar was dressed in black. Black trousers. A black leather coat. Even the cap on the burglar's head was black. It hid most of the face. The dark figure moved to the edge of the roof, and then, with one hand, reached down to the window. With one quick, expert movement, the window was opened. Then, with another quick, athletic movement, the figure moved off the roof and through the window. Not a sound was made. No alarms rang. The rain began to fall a little harder. It was now a few minutes after midnight.

Like a cat, black, silent and cruel, the midnight visitor passed painting after painting inside the dark gallery. The paintings were hanging on the walls. Many of them were famous. But the burglar was interested in only one. It was two floors below, at the end of a large room. The burglar reached it quickly. A small electric light in the burglar's hand showed the painter's name. He was a Dutch painter who had lived in the 1600s. He wasn't one of the most famous, but his work sold in New York, Paris, London and Hamburg for large amounts of money.

There was a wooden frame around the picture. It didn't take long to get the painting out of the frame. Then the painting was rolled up and put into a sack. There was another painting in the sack. The burglar put this second painting into the empty frame. It looked exactly like the first painting. Even an expert's eye couldn't tell the difference. Only chemical tests and X-rays could perhaps show that it was a forgery, a copy of the first painting and not the real thing. But nobody would ever make those tests. Nobody would know that a burglar at midnight had stolen the first painting and put a forgery in its place.

Everything was done quickly but expertly. The forgery was soon back on the wall, where the first painting had been before. It was in the same frame. There were no marks on the frame to show what had happened. Then the dark figure left as quickly and as silently as it had come. The same small lavatory window two floors above was used again. And again, no alarms rang. The burglar climbed through the window and onto the roof. The rain was still falling. For a moment the visitor stopped on the roof, reached down, and shut the window carefully and silently.

There was a tall tree next to the gallery. Part of it was very close to the roof. With the same strong, quick athletic movement, the burglar jumped from the roof and onto the tree.

The burglar reached the street below and stopped. In a dark side street, not far from the gallery, there was a small, fast sports car. The dark figure moved through the night and the rain, and got into the car. The sack, with the painting inside, was put on the back seat. Then the burglar took off the black cap. Blonde hair suddenly appeared. It was very long, and it fell around a woman's face. The burglar was a young woman!

She was around twenty-five. She was rather thin but there

was something strong and athletic in all her movements. She drove the car as expertly and as quickly as she had stolen the painting. The car raced along the wide boulevards and into the sleeping suburbs. It was now only half an hour past midnight. Soon she was on the road to Switzerland.

She was out of France before the sun came up. A sleepy man in a uniform on the French side only looked at her passport. He didn't even look at the sack on the back seat. Neither did the man on the Swiss side. She raced along the road from Basle to Zurich. It began to get lighter. The early winter sun rose slowly. The first snow hadn't fallen, but it was already very cold. She drove on. Less than two hours later she had reached Zurich. There was a large, old house on a hill above the lake there. The house had a balcony and an old man was waiting on it, in the cold, bright morning air. The girl parked outside the house and went up to the balcony.

"I did everything you wanted me to do. I followed your orders exactly," she said.

"And the painting?" the old man asked.

She pointed to the sack. The old man smiled for a moment.

"Let's go inside. It's cold. My arthritis is bothering me again," he said.

"Yes, father," the girl answered.

They went into a large, warm room. It was an artist's studio or workroom. There were paintbrushes and tubes of paint everywhere. The old man took the painting out of the sack and put it carefully on a large worktable. Then he turned on a strong light above the table. He studied the painting silently for several minutes.

"It's good. Artists then really knew how to paint," he said. "In fact," he went on, "it's almost as good as my copy of it."

Then he looked at the girl. She was tired.

"You'd better get some sleep, Karen. You'll have to take the painting to London tomorrow," he said.

CHAPTER TWO

A visit from Inspector Moore

Two men watched each other's movements carefully. They were both wearing white. Neither of them had shoes on. One of them was young and thin. The other was heavier. The heavier man suddenly shouted very loudly. He tried to hit the younger man with the side of his open hand. But the younger man suddenly stepped back. He brought his arm down on the other man's arm. Then, with his other hand, he hit the heavier man just above the neck. His hand wasn't closed but open. The fingers were held straight out. Just before he reached the man's neck, he stopped. A third man was watching. He was Japanese. The other two men weren't.

"No, not that way!" he shouted at the younger man. Both men stopped and moved back. The Japanese man was dressed in white, too. He showed the younger man the same movement again. The younger man watched carefully. He and the heavier man began to fight again. This time the younger man shouted very loudly. Once again, he tried to hit the other man but stopped just before he reached him.

"Better, Mr Rutland. Much better, but you still have a lot to learn. Karate isn't an easy art, even for an artist like yourself," the Japanese man said to the younger man.

The younger man smiled.

David Rutland lived in the centre of London, in Soho. He was learning the Japanese art of karate at a sports club. The sports club wasn't far from his own studio. He looked at the clock on the wall. He came to the club twice a week for an hour's lesson. The hour had just finished. He went to another room, washed and then changed into his own clothes. He was in a hurry that morning. He had a lot of work to do.

David did all sorts of work for film and television studios. After he had changed he hurried out of the sports club and across the busy street to his own studio. He had to finish a painting before noon. It was going to be used in a film about a Dutch painter. The painter had lived 400 years ago and the painting had to be in the correct style. He had almost finished it. Only a few things had to be done.

The company that was making the film was small. There were a lot of small film and television companies in Soho. The film director was coming to get the painting himself. David hoped the director would also bring the money. He needed it. Some of the small companies didn't pay on time. In fact, some of them never paid at all.

Just then the phone rang. At first David didn't answer it. He didn't want to stop working. The phone rang again, and then again. He put his paintbrush down angrily.

"Yes, who is it?" he shouted into the phone. He looked back at the painting. He was still thinking about it. The colours were very important. They had to be just right.

"Is that David Rutland?" a man's voice asked at the other end.

"Yes. That's right. Why?"

"My name's Moore. Inspector Moore. May I come to your studio? I'd like to have a few words with you." David suddenly stopped thinking about the painting.

"Inspector? What sort of inspector? A police inspector?" he asked.

"Yes, that's right. May I come to your studio now? It's very important."

David looked at his watch. He had to finish the painting quickly.

"Well, I'm very busy at the moment, and..." he began.

"I understand, Mr Rutland. It won't take long. I'll be right over," Moore said, and then hung up.

David went back to the painting.

"Why should a police inspector want to see me?" he asked himself. It was very strange, but David was used to strange things. The world of small film and television companies and poor artists was full of strange things. A few minutes later there was a knock at the door.

"Come in. It's open," David shouted. A tall man of about thirty-five stepped in. It was Moore.

The first thing David noticed about him was his eyes. They were very busy eyes. They looked all around the studio and at David himself. Moore seemed to be a man who noticed everything and forgot nothing.

"Sit down, Inspector. And please excuse me if I don't stop working. Someone's coming for this painting in a few minutes," David said. He turned back to the painting.

He could feel Moore's eyes on him.

"It's nice of you to see me when you're so busy," Moore said. David began working on the last part of the painting. He had to change some of the colours. He knew they weren't really right. But he hoped nobody would notice.

"And why do you want to see me? You still haven't told me," David asked without turning around.

There was a moment's silence.

"A nice painting. Dutch style, isn't it? Around 1600," Moore suddenly said. David stopped painting. He was surprised. He didn't think policemen were very interested in such things.

"Yes. How did you know?" he asked.

"It's part of my work. I have to know such things, Mr Rutland. You do these paintings for film companies, is that right?"

"Yes, when they want such things. But they don't very often. So I do all sorts of art work for them," David answered.

The inspector came closer to the painting.

"Hmm. That red," he said, and pointed to a woman's hat in the picture. "It's a bit modern, isn't it? I mean, Dutch painters didn't use that colour of red in 1600, did they?"

The inspector was right again. David was very surprised.

"Yes, but it doesn't have to be perfect. I mean, it's only for a film, that's all," he answered.

He suddenly remembered the time again. If he hurried, the painting would be ready in a few minutes. He went back to work and completely forgot about Moore for a time. Then, when the last part was finished, he stopped. Moore was still standing behind him. He was looking around the studio carefully.

"Now, perhaps you'll tell me why you're here. What can I do for you?" David asked. Moore didn't answer immediately. He looked at David as carefully as he had looked around the studio.

"I'm in a special part of the police. I'm interested in forgeries, the forgers themselves, and art thieves," he said.

"Forgers? Art thieves? People who forge and steal paintings, you mean? Are you saying that you think I'm…" David began, but Moore stopped him before he could finish.

"No, you haven't really understood, Mr Rutland. I don't think you steal or forge paintings, or anything like that. I only want you to help me."

David was more surprised than before.

"Me? Help you? Help the police? How?"

Before Moore could answer, there was another knock at the door. Then a young man came in without waiting. He had short hair and he was wearing a black suit and red shoes.

"Well, I hope the painting's ready now. I need it immediately!" the young man said. He had a loud, high voice, something like a woman's. It was the film director. He saw the painting and hurried over to it.

"Wonderful. Fabulous. First class!" he shouted without looking at it very carefully. He took it under his arm and turned to go again. David remembered the money. The film company hadn't paid him for the painting.

"Just a moment. What about the…"

The young film director didn't stop.

"Terribly sorry. Must hurry. Can't stop now. Must get back to the studio," he said.

"But you haven't paid me yet," David shouted.

"Bye!" the young man said in his high, woman's voice and hurried out of the room. He didn't even look back. David raced after him.

"But the money. You said you'd pay me as soon as the painting was finished," he shouted after him.

The director ran down the stairs and jumped into a car outside. There was a young woman in it. She was wearing sun glasses. It wasn't a very sunny day. The director closed the car door and started the engine.

"Bye bye!" he shouted again. Then he drove off. He and the girl were both laughing about something.

David went back to his studio. Inspector Moore was still there.

"As I was saying, Mr Rutland, we'd like you to help us." David looked at him.

"To do what?" he asked.

"To catch a forger. A very important forger. And some other people, too. And, by the way, we'd pay you. We'd pay you on time," Moore answered. There was a smile on his face.

David began to be more interested.

"Tell me more," he said.

Moore smiled again.

"Come to my office in New Scotland Yard," he answered.

CHAPTER THREE
The forger

When they got to the Inspector's office, Moore took out a large file and put it on the desk in front of David. The file was full of photographs, articles taken from newspapers and other things. Moore took out one of the newspaper articles and handed it to David. The date showed that the article was more than twenty years old. It was from an American newspaper.

David had heard Sharp's name before. Almost everyone in the art world had. People talked about him even now. Sharp had studied art in Holland and Italy. It was said that he had learned the secrets of the 'Old Masters' like Rembrandt, Rubens and Vermeer. He knew how to mix paints as they had done, and to make new paintings look very old. Even famous experts couldn't tell the difference. Only X-rays and chemical tests could do this. Sometimes even those weren't enough. Sharp knew all the secrets. He really was a great forger. Some people even said he was a great artist.

Moore took a photograph from the file. It was of a man about sixty-five. He was in a city street somewhere. Germany or Switzerland perhaps. The man didn't seem to know he was being photographed.

"That's what Sharp looks like now. The photograph was taken a few weeks ago in Zurich. That's where he lives," Moore said. He took a second photograph from the file. It was of a blonde woman, about twenty-five and rather beautiful. She was wearing some sort of white athletic costume.

"And that's Sharp's daughter, Karen. She's an Olympic gymnast."

"A what?" David asked.

"A gymnast. A first class gymnast. You know, they jump from bars and things like that. All for sport, of course."

David studied the two photographs.

"And why are you telling me this, Inspector?" he asked.

Moore got up and walked to the window. He seemed to be thinking carefully about what he was going to say. Finally he turned around.

"Sharp was sent to prison twenty years ago. Only for two years because the New York police couldn't prove very much against him. When he came out, he went back to Switzerland. He just disappeared. Nobody heard about him or knew exactly where he was or what he was doing. He didn't seem important any more. Then about three years ago some strange things began happening."

David looked up.

"Strange things? What do you mean?"

"A number of old Dutch paintings, all about 350 years old, were sold to rich collectors in the USA and South America. They weren't very famous works, but they were still worth a lot of money. Even second class 'Old Masters' are worth a lot of money these days. One day, not long ago, a collector in Argentina bought one of these paintings. Later, he found out that a museum in Amsterdam said they had the same painting."

"You mean, he found he'd bought a forgery?" David said.

"No, not quite. The Dutch police investigated. They found that the painting in the museum was a forgery. A very good one. But chemical tests proved that the forgery wasn't very old. The strange thing was that the museum had had the painting for over 100 years."

Suddenly David didn't understand. The whole story seemed impossible.

"In other words, the collector in Argentina had the original?"

"Exactly!" Moore answered.

"But how could the painting in the Amsterdam museum be a forgery if they had had it for so long? I mean, you said the forgery wasn't very old."

"We can't be sure. But we think that the original had been stolen from the museum. Someone had taken it and put a very good copy in its place. Then the original had been sold to the collector in Argentina. Later we found that the same thing had happened with a number of other paintings."

Moore stopped and looked at David carefully again. He seemed to be studying him. Then he went on.

"Only one person could have made such good copies of that painting and the others. We have to find out if he's behind all this. And we also have to find out how the paintings are stolen. We think we know who sells them."

He took out a third photograph from the file. A tall, well-dressed man was coming out of a London art gallery. He looked like a rich businessman. Moore pointed to the man and said, "Eric Orton, the owner of Orton International Art Gallery, here in London. A very powerful and rich man. Art is big business now, and he's in the centre of it."

Moore stopped and took a deep breath. He was coming to the point now, at last.

"Sharp is getting old. He has arthritis in his hands. We've heard he's looking for an assistant. But of course, he can't get one in the usual way. He has to be careful. He has to think that the assistant is also ready to forge paintings. We want you to become that assistant," he said.

"Me? But how? And why?"

"So that you can find out more about Sharp and who he's working with and how the paintings are stolen in the first place."

"But I can't just write to him, can I? I mean, I can't say 'Dear Sir, I want to become a forger like you. Please give me some work'," David said. Moore smiled.

"Of course not. We have a plan. The plan begins with Orton, here in London."

CHAPTER FOUR

At the art gallery

A few days later David found himself in front of the Orton International Art Gallery. It looked like a place for rich people, not for artists. A well-dressed woman was just coming out. She had a large diamond ring on her finger and there were diamonds round her neck, too. She was talking to a man in a dark suit. David could smell her perfume as she walked past. It was expensive perfume, the sort that comes in very small bottles and costs a very large amount of money.

"I do so love Rembrandt, don't you?" she was saying to the man. The man smiled. They both got into a large car that was waiting for them and drove away.

David stepped into the gallery. He could still smell the perfume of the woman who had gone out. He looked down at his old clothes. For a moment he didn't want to go any further. He stopped. There weren't many people in the gallery, but he could feel their eyes on him. He looked around. There were a number of paintings on the white walls. They were all at least 300 years old.

A young man came towards David. He looked carefully at David's old clothes and at the large leather case under his arm. It was the sort of case in which artists carry paintings.

"Yes, sir? May I help you?" the young man said in a low voice. He smiled carefully, too.

"Yes, I'd like to see Mr Orton. I have some paintings here," he said and pointed to the case. "I'd like to sell them."

The young man smiled carefully again.

"Mr Orton's a very busy man, I'm afraid. And we don't buy modern paintings here," he said in the same very low voice.

"Who said anything about modern paintings?" David asked in a loud voice. The other people in the gallery stopped talking and looked at him. The young man looked round at them.

"But I've just told you Mr Orton's very busy. I think you've come to the wrong place," he said. David spoke even more loudly.

"How do you know? You haven't seen the paintings!" He pointed to the case again. The young man opened his mouth to say something. David raised his voice a little more.

"I want to see Mr Orton. I don't want to talk to anybody but him!"

He looked around and saw a chair. He went to it and sat down.

"I can wait. I'm not in a hurry," David added.

He and the young man looked at each other in silence for a moment. The young man's smile had disappeared. He turned and went up some stairs that led to a kind of balcony. The balcony was at the end of the room. There seemed to be a kind of office there. A few minutes later the young man came back.

"Please follow me," he said in his low voice. They went up the stairs to the balcony. Then they went through an office. There was a woman sitting behind a typewriter there. They went past her and into another room. It was a very large room and there was a man behind a very large desk in it. The man didn't look up. The young man said nothing more. After he had taken David inside, he left again.

The man at the desk was about forty-five. He was wearing a dark suit and a very white shirt. He was also wearing glasses and the glasses had a metal frame.

David stood there in silence. The man hadn't looked up yet. He was reading a letter. Almost a minute went by.

"Yes? What is it? What do you want?" the man finally said. He still didn't look up from the letter. David walked towards the desk.

"I have two paintings here. I think you'll be interested in them," he said. "You are Mr Orton, aren't you?" he asked.

At last the man looked up. He had cold blue eyes behind the glasses. He studied David for several seconds before he answered.

"Yes," he said.

David took the paintings from the case. They were both forgeries. David had painted them himself. He had signed the name of a Dutch painter on them. The painter had died more than 350 years ago. He wasn't one of the most famous artists of the time. And the forgeries weren't too good. It was all part of the plan.

"But will the plan work?" David wondered.

Orton looked at the paintings for a few seconds.

"Where did you get them?" he asked.

"That's my business," David said.

"It's my business, too, if you want me to buy them," Orton answered. Again there was silence. Orton waited.

"They belonged to someone in my family," David answered.

"Leave the paintings here for a few days. I'll have to study them carefully. Very carefully," Orton said.

"No. I can't do that. I need the money. I need it now." Orton looked back at the letter again.

"Leave them here or get out, and take the paintings with you!" he said without looking up. David didn't seem very sure of himself.

"Why can't you tell me now if you want them?" he asked.

"Please don't waste my time. If you want to sell the paintings, leave them here. And leave your name with the girl outside. If you don't want to do that, get out!"

Orton spoke quickly without raising his voice. David didn't seem to know what to do. Then he turned. He left the room. The paintings were still there.

CHAPTER FIVE

Orton

There was a knock at the door. It was a few days later and it was late in the evening. David was in his studio. When he opened the door, two men were standing there. One was short. The other was taller. Both men were strangers.

"Is your name Rutland?" the shorter one asked.

"Yes. Why?"

"I'd like to come in. All right?" the short man said. He walked past before David could answer. The taller man waited outside.

"Get your coat," the short man said after he had looked round the studio for a few moments.

"I don't understand. What do you mean?" David asked. He didn't like the look of the man.

"Someone wants to see you," the man answered.

"Who?"

"Harry!" the short man suddenly shouted. The tall, silent man came in. He closed the door, crossed his arms and looked at David coldly. He didn't speak.

"Just get your coat and everything will be all right," the short man said.

David stared at the two men. They stared back at him.

"Don't give us any trouble," the short man said. David got his coat.

They got into a car. It was big and fast. The tall man drove. The other one sat in the back with David.

"Where are we going?" David asked.

"You'll find out," the short man said. The tall man still

had said nothing.

"Doesn't your friend ever talk?" David pointed to him.

"He isn't paid to talk. He's paid to do other things," the short man said. They drove on. In silence. Not a word was said.

The tall man drove fast. Very fast. He didn't seem to notice the other cars on the road. But they noticed him. They almost seemed to get out of his way, just as smaller animals get out of the way of bigger, more dangerous ones. Soon they had left the city. They were out in the country, but David didn't know where. It was dark. They passed some road signs. But they were driving so fast that he couldn't read them.

Almost an hour went by. Nobody spoke. The only sound was that of the car's powerful engine. They turned into a narrow country road and drove along it. They seemed to be among a lot of trees. It got even darker. After a few minutes they seemed to come out of the trees. Ahead of them, at the end of the narrow road, David could see a large house. It looked very old. There were lights on in all the windows. They drove up to it and stopped. A party seemed to be going on inside. David could hear music and people laughing.

"We're here. Get out," the short man said.

"Where's 'here'?" David asked.

"Don't ask questions. Just follow me," the short man answered.

He led David through a small side door. They walked up some steps and into a library. Everything in the library looked very expensive. There was a large desk at one end of the room and there were some paintings on the walls. The short man went to the desk and picked up a small telephone.

"I've got Rutland," he said into it.

Then he sat down. David was still standing. The short man watched him coldly. He never took his eyes off him.

A few minutes later the door opened and a man stepped in. It was Orton. He was dressed for the party. He looked at the short man. The short man stood up.

"I'll be outside," he said to Orton. Then he left. He closed the door silently. Orton and David were alone.

"I'm glad you decided to come," Orton said.

"I didn't decide. Your friends decided for me."

Orton took a long white cigarette from an expensive-looking cigarette case. He didn't offer one to David.

"I wanted to see you about your two paintings," Orton said. He went to the end of the room and turned on a light. The paintings were there, against the wall. The light shone down on them.

"Why was I brought here? Why did you have to see me about them in the evening?" David asked.

Orton didn't answer. He stood there, looking down at the paintings. David came closer.

"Well? What do you think of them?" David demanded loudly. Orton seemed to be thinking for a moment. Then he looked up.

"What do I think of them?" He seemed to be thinking about the question very carefully. "Yes. What do I think of them?" he repeated. Then, in answer to the question, he suddenly kicked one of the paintings. He kicked it very hard. His foot went through it. It left a very large hole.

"That's what I think of your paintings!" he said. He smiled coldly. Then he waited to see what David would do.

David stared at Orton. He opened his mouth to say something. But he couldn't think of any words. He shut his mouth again. Orton laughed and then pointed to the table at the other end of the room.

"There's a telephone there. Why don't you use it?" he said.

"What... what do you mean?"

"Phone the police. Tell them what I've just done. I've just kicked a hole in your painting. And it's very old, isn't it? Painted around 1600, wasn't it, Mr Rutland?"

It was the first time Orton had used David's name. He seemed to be laughing at David. He thought he had power over David now. And he was a man who enjoyed having power over other people. David could see that.

"A forgery, Mr Rutland. Both paintings are forgeries!

Rather poor forgeries! And you're a forger!"

For the first time Orton raised his voice. For the first time he seemed angry. David said nothing. He waited. He wanted to see what Orton would do.

"But why did you bring them to me, Rutland? Why to me? That's what I want to know," Orton demanded.

Again David opened his mouth to say something. And again it seemed he couldn't think of anything. He shut his mouth, opened it, then shut it again. Orton waited. Then he went to the door and opened it. The short man came in. The two of them looked at David coldly and silently.

"I want answers, Rutland. I want them now!" Orton suddenly said.

"I... uh... I..." David began, and then stopped.

Orton looked at the short man. The short man came close to David and then raised his hand. He hit David across the face.

"Why did you bring them to me?" Orton demanded again.

"I took them to five different galleries. Your gallery was the last one. None of the others wanted to buy them," David finally said.

It was true. It would have seemed very strange if David had gone only to Orton. David knew that. The other galleries hadn't been very interested. One had made an offer, but David had asked for more money. A second gallery had said they were interested only in modern art. The third gallery hadn't wanted to buy at all. Neither had the fourth. David knew Orton could find out all these things.

"Perhaps you're working with the police," Orton suddenly said. David looked very surprised.

"Just give me back my paintings and I'll go," he said.

He went to the end of the room to get the two pictures. When he turned, the short man was behind him. He pushed David against the wall. David dropped the paintings and pushed back. Then the short man hit him in the stomach very hard. David fell to the floor.

He lay there for a few seconds. He couldn't breathe.

Finally he got to his feet slowly.

"I could phone the police now. Forgery's a very bad thing. You could be sent to prison for a long time," Orton said. David slowly got his breath back.

"All right. Go on. Phone the police. That is, if you're sure I'm not working with them," he said with difficulty.

"You seem to know something about the way the old Dutch painters worked. Where did you learn?" Orton demanded.

"That's my business. Just let me go. Or call the police, and stop playing games with me," David answered.

Orton stared at him for a long time. He seemed to be thinking. There was silence for a few minutes. The short man never took his eyes off David. Orton sat down behind the desk. He finished another cigarette.

"I can give you some work. Are you interested?" he suddenly asked. Again, David looked very surprised.

"What kind of work?"

Orton didn't answer immediately. He thought for a moment. Finally he looked up at David.

"You'd be paid for it. You'd be paid very well. You'd be helping someone. But you'd have to leave England for a few months. And you'd have to do better work than that." He pointed to the two paintings. "But perhaps you could learn to do better work," he added. He smiled and waited.

"What if I say 'no'? What if I tell the police you've offered me work? What if I tell them you want me to forge paintings?" David asked angrily.

Orton smiled again.

"Who would believe you? You're a forger already. Not even a very good one. I have the proof there. If you tell the police anything, I'll tell them you tried to sell me those paintings. You'll be sent to prison."

CHAPTER SIX
Followed

That night David lay awake for a very long time. He was thinking. He had got into this thing without asking himself the right questions. Did he really want to work for the police? What would happen to him if Orton found out? He knew the answer to the last question already.

He hadn't known there were men like Orton in the art world. He hadn't known that such a man would have friends like George, the short man, and Harry, the tall silent one. It was true that they were in the shadows of Orton's world. But they were there all the same. And there were a lot of shadows in that world. Art was big business. There was a lot of money in it. Orton was the sort of man who would do anything for money and power. That was why he had men like George and Harry. David slept very badly that night.

The next morning, when he got up, he looked out of the window. Harry, the tall man, was standing across the street. He was staring at David's window. David hadn't phoned Inspector Moore. It was dangerous to use his own phone. It was dangerous, in fact, to try to phone Moore at all. But he had to do so. There was a small coffee shop down the street. David often had breakfast there. He went out. Harry followed him at a distance. He knew David could see him. But he didn't seem to care. He followed David to the coffee shop. David sat down at a table and ordered some breakfast. Harry came in and sat at another table. He didn't speak to David.

There were some narrow stairs that led to a lavatory.

There was a phone there, just outside the door marked 'Gentlemen'. Harry couldn't see him there. David got up and pointed to the lavatory sign.

"I'm going there for a few minutes. Do you want to come with me?" he asked Harry in a loud voice.

Harry looked at him coldly. He didn't answer. David went through the door and down the narrow stairs. He got to the phone, looked round and picked it up. Moore answered the call.

"Orton wants me to leave England for a few months. I'm sure he wants me to go to Switzerland to help Sharp," David said. Then he told Moore about George and Harry.

"I think I know those two. They're dangerous. Very dangerous," Moore said.

"I know," David answered.

"Well, then. Be careful!"

"It's a bit late to tell me that now, isn't it?" David said.

He went back up the stairs and sat down at the table. He finished his breakfast in a hurry. Harry sat not far away, watching him.

Bruno Sharp's hands were hurting him again. It was the arthritis. Sometimes the old man found it difficult to hold the brushes between his fingers. His daughter, Karen, came into the large old house on the hill above the lake of Zurich. He looked at her. She smiled a bright, healthy smile. Sometimes he wished that he was young again. His daughter had all her life in front of her. Sadly, most of his life was behind him.

"Where have you been?" he asked.

"Driving," she answered.

She often went driving in her sports car. And she always drove very fast. She seemed to enjoy danger. Sometimes Sharp couldn't really understand his daughter. He didn't really understand why she stayed with him, why she helped him.

"We'll be having a visitor. A young man," he said.

"Why?"

"Orton's sending him here to help me. I need someone to

help me. It's the arthritis."

"Someone came to help you last year. Do you remember? Do you remember what happened to him?" she asked.

Sharp didn't answer.

"Those two terrible men, George and Harry! I hope I never see them again," she said.

"That's Orton's business. Not mine. I have nothing to do with such things," Sharp answered. He looked out of the window. The first snow was falling. He hated the winter. Old men often die in the winter.

David was followed everywhere for a few days. It was always George or Harry. One of them was always behind him or standing outside, staring up at his window. One morning he came out of his studio and walked across the street. George was there.

"Don't you ever get tired?" David asked him.

"Tired of what?" George said.

"Of following me everywhere."

"We just want you to understand," George answered.

"Understand what?"

"That we're watching you. That we're keeping an eye on you."

David looked up and down the street.

"Where's the other animal?" he asked.

George stared at him coldly.

"What do you mean, 'animal'?" he asked.

"Perhaps 'dog' is a better word. That's what you and Harry are, aren't you? Orton's two watchdogs. Wild watchdogs," David said.

It was clear from the look in George's eyes that he hated David. But David hated him, too. And he didn't care if he knew. David remembered what had happened in the library. He turned and walked away.

At the end of the week, there was another knock on David's door. It was Harry, the tall one. He handed David a plane ticket. Then, without saying anything, he walked away. The ticket was for the next day. It was a one-way ticket to Zurich.

CHAPTER SEVEN

The Lady With Green Eyes

Something very important happened the day David flew to Zurich. The British National Art Gallery bought a famous old painting from a museum in Amsterdam. The painting was called *The Lady With Green Eyes* and there was a very strange story about it.

In 1635 a young Dutch painter had died. His name was Jan de Groot. He hadn't painted very much in his life, but people already spoke of him as a great artist. A friend of de Groot's wrote a book about the artist and his work in 1638. He wrote about every painting de Groot had done in his short life. The first strange thing was that one of the paintings couldn't be found later. The writer said that it was a picture of a young woman. He wrote about the dress she was wearing in the painting, and also about a few other things. The woman was wearing a ring, and the ring had a green stone in it. The woman's eyes were green, too.

For a long time people wondered about the painting. How had it disappeared? Who had it? Some said that it had disappeared in a fire. The fire had broken out in de Groot's home a short time after he had died.

But more than 350 years later, the painting was found again. And in many ways this was the strangest part of the story. It was found in the house of an old lady in Amsterdam. She had died, and one of her nephews had found it in an old bedroom which she never used. He had come from America to visit his aunt. When he got there she had already died. She lived alone in the house and never went out. She was a very strange old woman. Her nephew sold the painting to the museum for a very large amount of money. That was ten years ago.

Some experts didn't really think it was de Groot's work at all. Not at first, at least. The writer of the book in 1638 hadn't said very much about it. But it was a very good painting. Chemical tests and X-rays were used. It seemed it really was more than 350 years old. The paints were exactly the sort of paints that artists had used then. And they were very hard, just like paints that had had 350 years to dry out. Everything else about the painting was right. The frame was made in exactly the same way that frames were made 350 years ago. The canvas, or cloth the picture was painted on, was the right sort, too. Finally, it was accepted that it really was de Groot's work. People noticed the strange colour of the woman's eyes. They were green, but a very strange green. And so they began to call the painting *The Lady With Green Eyes*.

A few years later something happened to the old woman's nephew, the man who had found the painting. His body was found in a canal in Amsterdam. Who had killed him? And why? These questions were still not answered.

The day David left for Zurich, the newspapers were full of the story. Ten years after the man had found it, eight years after he had died, the painting had come to Britain. But David didn't read the stories in the papers very carefully. He was thinking about other things.

Inspector Moore was reading the newspaper stories when the phone rang in his office at New Scotland Yard. It was a detective at London Airport.

"Rutland's plane has just taken off," the detective said.

"All right. I'll tell the Zurich police."

Moore put the phone down. He was thinking about the painting. He had been interested in it for a very long time.

National Buys Lady
With Green Eyes

In the house on the lake, Sharp was trying to work. The arthritis in his hands was worse again. He was getting old. He wondered how much time he had left. Karen came in.

"Have you seen the English papers?" she asked.

She gave him one. There was a photograph of de Groot's painting on the front page.

"I think I'd better go to the airport now," Karen said.

"Yes. He'll be arriving soon." He didn't look up at her. He was looking at the photograph. It didn't give a very good idea of the painting. But Sharp didn't need a photograph. He could almost see the painting inside his head. He could even see her eyes, and their colour. A person with the same colour of eyes had died one cold night in New York. Karen had only been a child then.

Sharp read the newspaper article very carefully. Karen hadn't left yet. She watched him.

"You seem very surprised, father. Is it something to do with the painting?"

"Yes. I knew the British wanted the picture. But I had hoped they wouldn't buy it. Not so soon. I need more time."

Karen came closer. She didn't understand. There were so many things she didn't understand about him.

"Why? Time to do what?" she asked. She could see he didn't want to answer.

"You'd better go to the airport now," he said.

She repeated the question. He walked to the window and looked at the lake. Then he looked at his hands.

"I'm more than a forger. I'm more than that!" he suddenly said. He went on, "When I die, people won't remember me. Or if they do, they'll say I wasn't really an artist. They'll say I could only copy other people's work. But an artist, a real artist does new things. He shows people things only he can see. He takes something that is dead, something that is paint and shadow, and he puts life into it. He puts his own life into it! His own life!"

Sharp wasn't really saying this to Karen. He was saying it to himself.

"But what's that got to do with the article in the newspaper?" Karen asked.

"I can do more than copy other people's work! I can and I have!" he said.

Karen began to get angry. She still didn't understand. When she asked clear questions, she didn't get a clear answer from him.

"You never really tell me anything, father. I sometimes don't know why I stay with you!"

Sharp looked at her and laughed.

"Then I'll tell you why. Because you like danger. You want excitement. That's fine now, but one day you'll understand that there's more to life than that."

CHAPTER EIGHT

The painting lesson

Someone was calling David's name over the loudspeakers at Zurich Airport. He had just landed.

"Will Mr David Rutland please go to the information desk," the voice was saying.

A girl was waiting there for him.

"My name's Karen Sharp. I'll drive you to our house," she said.

They got into a sports car and drove away. Karen didn't say anything. David noticed her hands. They weren't very large, and the fingers were long. But they seemed very strong. She drove very fast but also very expertly. In a way, he thought, she was like a cat. She wasn't very large, but she was very quick in all her movements. She never wasted a movement, either. Then he remembered what Moore had said about her. She was a first class athlete, a gymnast. He had once seen another woman like her. In the karate club in London, they had shown a film. His karate teacher had said, "Watch this girl. She isn't big and doesn't look strong. But she is. She's strong because she knows exactly how to use her body. And she uses the power of thought, too. She has thought about each movement before she makes it."

In the film she fought a much larger man. It was only a film, but David had learned a lot from it. The girl knew exactly what to do. She knew which points of the man's body to hit.

They came to a large old house on a hill above the lake.

There was a man waiting on the balcony. He was studying David. It was Sharp. He looked older than in the photograph that Moore had shown David. He smiled.

"Come in. We'll have some lunch together." They sat down at a large table in a small, sunny room. The cold winter sunshine fell through a large window. He could see the lake clearly, and the very blue sky, and the mountains in the distance. While they were eating, David studied Karen and her father. They seemed strangely different. They didn't look like father and daughter at all. Sharp noticed him. He seemed to read David's thoughts.

"She doesn't look very much like me, does she? No. She looks like her mother."

"And... uh... where's her mother,... your wife, I mean?" David asked. For a second a strange, dark look came over Sharp's face.

"Dead. She's been dead for a long time," he said.

Nobody said anything more during lunch.

After lunch, Sharp stood up.

"Come with me. I want to see what you can do," he said.

He led David into the studio. David noticed that the studio was really two rooms. One of them was separated from the other by a door.

"This is where you will work. I'll do all my work in there," Sharp said, and pointed to the other room.

"Sit down over there."

He pointed to a place near the window, in front of a large worktable. Then he went to the other room. He took a key out of his pocket and opened the door. David saw that only Sharp could go into the second room. He went in and came out with a pencil drawing. It was of a woman, and she was carrying a basket of fruit.

"Paint from the drawing," Sharp said.

There were brushes and paint on the worktable. There was also a canvas. Sharp had placed it on an easel, so everything was ready for David to start painting.

David did the body of the woman first, without her clothes. Sharp watched every movement of David's brush.

When David had done that, he began to paint the woman's clothes.

"Good!" Sharp said. "At least you learned that much in art school. You must feel that there's really a body behind the clothes in a painting. You must feel that the body has bones, and blood in it. That's what the old painters did. The real artists!"

Sharp talked while David was working. It was clear that he hated everything that was modern. To him, all real art had stopped at the beginning of the twentieth century, or before. At one point he got up and began to walk around. He seemed strangely excited.

"When I was young, I tried to show the world what real art is. I tried to paint in the way the real artists of the past had done – Leonardo, Masaccio, Rembrandt, Vermeer. I didn't copy. But I painted in the same way. And people laughed at me! They laughed!"

There was anger in his voice now.

Before David had finished the painting, Sharp told him to stop.

"You needn't finish it. It's only an exercise," he said. But he still looked at it very carefully.

"Not bad. The colours are all wrong, of course. But I can take care of that part of it. Now I want you to do something that's more difficult. Far more difficult," he said.

He drew the figure of another woman. A child was sitting on her knee. The woman had one arm around the child. The other was raised in front of the child.

"Now paint the woman's hand. Hands are really difficult, more difficult than bodies in many ways. Remember! She's the child's mother. She loves the child. She doesn't want anything to happen to the child. You must show this when you paint the hand!" he said.

David began. He had done such exercises in art school, but he had never liked them. He was far more interested in more modern things.

"No! Not like that!" Sharp said after a few minutes. He pointed to the woman's thumb.

"That thumb is only a shape and some colour. That's all it is, and it isn't enough. I can't feel the bone! I must feel the bone even if I can't see it!"

David did the thumb again, but Sharp was still unhappy.

"All right. Forget the thumb. Do the other fingers," he said. David tried but he was beginning to feel very tired.

"Remember the mother's feelings. Those feelings must be seen in the hand. There must be fear and love there!"

When David had finished, Sharp stepped back and studied it from a distance.

"No. I can't feel the life in that hand. I can't feel that there are bones and nerves and blood in that hand!" Then he looked at his watch.

"It's late, you must be tired. You have a great deal to learn, but at least you can draw. We'll start tomorrow. You'll work in here, and I'll work there," he said, and pointed to the other room again. It was the room only Sharp could go into. Sharp smiled. For a moment there was a kind look in his face again.

They had dinner. Nobody said very much. But all kinds of thoughts raced through David's head. Why was a man like Sharp working with a man like Orton? Sharp was clearly interested in more than money. And then there was another question. Moore had spoken about a 'contact' in Zurich. The 'contact' was the person from the Zurich police. This person would give information to David and get it from him. But how would this person contact David? He had to be very careful. Sharp was perhaps an artist, but behind him, in the shadows, there were men like Orton. And George and Harry.

CHAPTER NINE

The other room

Work really started the next day. It was a very strange way to work.

Sharp never allowed David to watch him at work. He was doing a kind of seventeenth century Dutch painting. It was the kind called a drinking scene. Three men were sitting at a table. One of them was drinking from a large glass. The other men were laughing. A woman was standing at the table with a kind of wine bottle in her hands. Sharp did most of the painting in the other room. He brought the picture into David's room and then pointed to a few small parts of the picture.

"Finish this part, the man's hat," he said. He gave him other small parts like that to do.

The paints were difficult to work with, too. Sharp always mixed them himself. And again, he never allowed David to watch him. David had to work very quickly because the paints dried very fast. And when they had dried, they were very very hard. Usually it took years and years for paints to get so hard. Sharp always gave him very small amounts of them. He knew exactly how much David would need each time. He never gave him too much and never too little. Sharp never allowed David to come into the other room.

But David could still see things that were wrong about the painting. For example, there were no cracks in the paint. Old paintings always have thousands of such cracks, just like the lines on an old man's face.

And the paints themselves still looked far too bright. After a few hundred years, even the brightest paints get dark. He said something about this to Sharp.

"I'll take care of all that. I'll take care of it later," he said.

"How?" David asked.

Sharp didn't answer.

David had to get all the information he could about Sharp, and about the ways he worked. He saw it wasn't going to be easy.

A few days later, they were working when the telephone rang. Karen wasn't there to answer it. The phone was in another room. Sharp came out of his part of the studio to answer it. He had to come out quickly. David heard him talking, and he seemed to be in the middle of a long conversation. He walked to the door of Sharp's studio very quietly and looked in.

The first thing he noticed was the smell. Sharp's studio smelt like a flower shop. Then David saw why. There were a lot of flowers on the worktable in the centre of the room. But it was clear Sharp wasn't going to paint them. He had cut them up. David wondered why.

Then he noticed the oven. It wasn't really like a kitchen oven, the sort people use to bake bread and cakes. It was much larger than that.

"Why does Sharp have an oven in here?" David asked himself. He looked back and listened. Sharp was still talking on the phone. He went into the room again. There were also some shaving brushes on the table. They were the type men had used fifty years ago. He picked one of them up and felt the hair. It was a natural, animal hair. And it was the same as the hair of the paintbrushes.

In the far corner, there was a picture. David had been sure that Sharp was painting another one. This was it. But he couldn't see what it was. There was a piece of cloth over it. David wondered why Sharp hadn't given him parts of this second painting to do. He was going to walk over to it, but then he stopped. Sharp seemed to be finishing the phone conversation! He was saying something like "Goodbye" in German. David got back to his place in the other room just before Sharp came in again. Sharp looked around. He suddenly noticed that the door to his own studio was still open. His eyes travelled to the door, back to David, and then to the door again. David didn't seem to notice. He didn't even look up at Sharp.

That afternoon, David went for a walk. A young woman with two children came towards him on the empty street. She was talking to the children in Swiss German. One of the children rushed past him. She followed it. But when she passed by she suddenly said clearly, but not loudly, in English, "Mr Rutland. Be in the park around the corner. Tuesday or Thursday afternoon. 3.30. Don't look at me! Keep walking!"

She seemed to be talking to the child, but she wasn't.

CHAPTER TEN

The woman in the park

He went for a walk the next Thursday afternoon. The park was also on a hill. It looked down on the lake and a busy road that led out of the centre of Zurich. There was a museum in the park. It seemed to have mostly Asian art in it. David sat down on one of the benches. It was very cold. The park was empty.

A few minutes later he heard the sound of children's voices. They were playing with a dog. There were two of them, a boy and a girl. There was a young woman with them. She seemed to be taking care of them. It was the same young woman. She walked up the hill a bit. David followed her. It was a good place to talk. They could see anybody who was coming, and there was a large tree. It hid them partly.

"I'm your contact here in Zurich. My name's Jenny," she said. Jenny was an English policewoman. She was working with the Zurich police.

"We mustn't be seen together. Be very careful," she said.

"It's all right. Sharp's in his studio. His daughter isn't even in Zurich today," David said.

"There may be other people watching," Jenny answered. David looked at her in surprise.

"Other people? Who?" he asked.

"George and Harry."

"But they're in London!" he said.

"No. Orton sends them here, and to other places, too. They keep an eye on everybody working for him," she answered.

They had very little time to talk, but David learned a little bit more about Sharp.

"Sharp does two kinds of work, we think," Jenny said. "First, he does forgeries of pictures in museums all over the world. Then the originals are stolen. Sharp's forgeries are put in their place. Orton sells the originals to people in South America and the United States."

"But what if the buyers find out that the originals really belong to the museums?" David asked.

"If they do, Orton has a very good answer. He can prove that he sold the original and that the museum has a forgery. Sharp's forgeries are very good. The museum can't prove that it hasn't had the forgery for hundreds of years."

"And what about the second kind of work?" David asked.

"They're different paintings. Sharp sometimes does completely new pictures, but in the style of artists 350 years ago. Again, they're never the most famous artists. That would be too dangerous. Then Orton says these are paintings that have just been found, or that he has just bought them."

Jenny looked around. They were still alone in the park. Only they and the children were there.

"Listen carefully," she said. "This may be the only time we can talk like this. Try to come here on Tuesday or Thursday afternoon every week at this time. Sit over there." She pointed to a bench. There was another bench behind it. The two were back to back.

"The children will always be with me. I'll talk to you but it must seem that I'm really talking to the children," she added.

"But what if I want to say something to you?" David asked.

"Then talk to the children, too. Or to the dog. But never to me! Do you understand?"

She wanted to leave. But there was one last thing she had to tell David.

"What did Moore tell you about a man called Monti, Alessandro Monti?" she asked him.

"Monti? Who's he?"

"He isn't. He was!" she said.

It took David a few seconds to understand.

"You mean... he's dead?"

"Yes. We think so. But we've never found the body. He did some paintings for Orton in Italy. Then he came here last year, to help Sharp. One day George and Harry came here, too. The next day Monti disappeared." She stopped and looked around at the park.

"But why was he killed?" David asked.

"We don't know. But we'd like to find out. You can be sure of one thing. Orton was behind it. If Monti was killed, Orton gave the orders."

She looked around again, and then up at the sky. It was getting very cold. There was a lot of snow up in the grey clouds.

"Be very careful, Mr Rutland," she said before she left. "The same thing that happened to Monti could also happen to you."

David watched her go. He stood there, thinking. The wind got colder. Heavy snow began to fall. He suddenly felt very alone.

In the weeks that followed, Sharp gave David more and more to do. They were always very small things, but very difficult. But Sharp still didn't allow David to come into his own part of the studio, where the oven was. And he still mixed the paints himself. Karen was often away. Sharp never said where she was, or what she was doing. David went to the park on Tuesdays and Thursdays. Jenny sat down on the bench behind him.

"Karen's in London," she said. It seemed she was speaking to one of the children. That was all she said.

Something happened the next Thursday that was very strange. Jenny came into the park but walked past the bench. She didn't sit down. She didn't even look at him. He had the feeling that she had seen something or someone. He looked around but didn't notice anything unusual. The park was empty. It almost always was, at that time of the day, and in the cold weather.

"Why didn't she sit down behind me?" David asked himself.

That evening, after he had finished the day's work, he went to his room and lay down. Then he heard the sound of a car on the street below. It stopped in front of the house. Someone got out. He went to the window and looked down. It was Karen. She had come back from London. David's room was on the top floor of the house. He opened the door a bit and listened. He could just hear what was said downstairs.

Karen went into the living room. Sharp was still there. For a while they talked in low voices. David couldn't understand anything. But then their voices became more excited and rose. Luckily, they were speaking English. Karen had been born and brought up in America. She didn't know Swiss German very well, and always used English when she wanted to say something important. And this clearly was important.

"But it's impossible, father! I've seen the gallery! I've just come from London!" he heard her shout.

Then Sharp closed the living room door and David could hear no more. He went down the stairs silently. When he was halfway down, he stopped. He was close enough to catch a few words. They were still talking loudly.

"It isn't a small museum in Paris or Amsterdam," Karen was saying. "It's the British National Art Gallery. There are guards everywhere. And it's a famous painting, too. One of the most famous in the world!"

Sharp tried to say something.

"But you don't understand. I don't want you to..."

"No, father. Listen to me for once. Orton won't help you, either. The painting's too famous. He could never sell it. People would ask too many questions."

Sharp seemed to get very angry.

"This has nothing to do with Orton," he shouted. "That

man has made too much money from my work already!"

They began to speak more quietly. Once David heard him ask, "Who said I wanted to sell the painting?"

David turned and went upstairs again after a few more minutes. He had just got to his room when Karen said loudly, "It's impossible, but if you really want me to, I'll try!"

CHAPTER ELEVEN
Sharp's secret

A few days went by. David was beginning to get to know Sharp a little better. Another Tuesday came, and he went to the park again. This time Jenny wasn't there at all. The next day he started on another painting.

They had finished the first painting, the drinking scene. But there was still one thing wrong with it. It wasn't cracked. The style was right, but because there were no cracks in the paint, it still didn't look old enough. When he said something about it, Sharp answered, "I'm going to take care of that this afternoon."

They had already started on a second picture. This one was a winter scene on a Dutch canal. The winter sun shone through dark grey clouds. People were skating on the ice of the canal. There was snow everywhere. Sharp had already done part of the painting and had told David to finish parts of the skating figures.

David had also found out why Sharp made paintbrushes from the old shaving brushes. The shaving brushes were made with a certain kind of animal hair. It was very difficult to get. The hair was the same kind the old Italian and Dutch painters had used for their paintbrushes. Sharp had to use the same kind of hair. If an expert found a modern hair in one of his paintings, he would know it was a forgery. Experts looked for such things when they examined pictures.

That afternoon, Sharp was working in his own part of the studio, behind the closed door. He had still not allowed David to come into the room. David was working on the skating figures. Suddenly, from the other room, Sharp called out.

"Come in here, please. Hurry!"

His voice sounded strange and weak. David opened the door. He had no time to look around. Sharp was sitting down. His face looked very white, strangely white. He was having difficulty in breathing.

"There are some pills in that desk. Get them," he said in the same weak voice. He pointed to a writing desk near the wall.

David found a bottle of small white pills and gave them to Sharp.

"Water. I need some water. Hurry!" he said.

David got some. Sharp's hands were shaking. He took the water and the pills quickly.

"A doctor! Perhaps you ought to have a doctor!" David said. Sharp shook his head.

"Just wait here a moment," he said.

Suddenly a bell went off. It sounded like an electric egg-timer. The sound had come from the oven. Sharp was still too weak to stand up.

"Open the oven," he said.

David did so. The drinking scene was inside. It was on a special metal frame.

"Quickly! There's not much time. Take the painting off the frame and wrap it around that tube. Hurry!"

Sharp pointed to a metal tube on the worktable. It was very thick. He stood up and began to help David a little. The painting was rolled around the tube and then Sharp pointed to a jar. It was full of a thick kind of oil paint, but the paint itself had no colour.

Sharp began to rub the colourless oil paint into the cracks of the picture. He told David to do the same. The great heat of the oven had made a great number of cracks. They were very small. Still more appeared when the painting was rolled tightly on the tube. When this was done, the painting was taken off the tube and laid flat on the large worktable. It was face down.

"Press down on the painting. Press down hard, all over," Sharp said. After they had done this they turned the painting over again. David saw that they had pressed all the extra colourless paint out of the cracks. Sharp wiped it away from the painting with a clean cloth. Then David hung it up on another special metal frame.

"In a few days it'll be ready for a wooden frame," Sharp said. "That's very important. The wooden frame has to be just right. If there's anything wrong with it, experts will know it's a forgery."

David looked at the painting. It was clearly not one that was already in a museum somewhere. It wasn't going to be put in place of an original. It was going to be one of Orton's 'finds'. Orton would say that it had disappeared hundreds of years ago.

Sharp looked a little better. The terrible whiteness had gone from his face. But he was still very weak.

"What was wrong? What happened?" David asked. Sharp said nothing. He only pointed to his heart.

"Shall I get a doctor now?"

Sharp shook his head.

"A doctor can't help. He would only tell me something I already know."

"Shall I tell Karen?"

Sharp shook his head again.

"She must know nothing of this. Nothing!" Then he added, "Let's have something to drink. Would you like a cup of tea? A very special tea. It comes from a distant part of China and it's only drunk on special occasions."

David was very surprised. Sharp had never been so friendly before. It seemed that he wanted to talk to someone. They drank the tea together. It was very good, with a particularly delicate flavour.

"You can't buy this in the shops. It comes from my wife's family," Sharp suddenly said. David looked at him. Sharp had never spoken of his wife before.

"Your wife's family?" he asked.

"Yes. Her father had a tea and coffee business. He imported fine teas like this but this was his own favourite which he didn't sell to anyone."

His face went dark again for a moment. He stopped. Then he added, "My wife and I lived in America through the worst years. She died there, when Karen was still very young."

He said nothing more for a few seconds. He seemed to be thinking. Then he looked at David very carefully.

"I'm an old man. I haven't much time left. But I've got a few very important things to do. You'll have to help me. I'll have to give you a lot more to do now."

David was beginning to like Sharp, even if he didn't really understand him. Suddenly he thought of Moore and what Moore wanted him to do.

"Perhaps you shouldn't tell me too many of your secrets," he said. He said it quickly, almost without thinking. And he didn't really know why he had said it. But Sharp didn't seem to notice anything strange. He laughed.

"I have more secrets than most men. When I die, those secrets will die with me. But perhaps you'll learn a few of them."

Suddenly he looked very weak again. He began to get up. David stood up to help him, but Sharp shook his head.

"I'm all right!"

He walked slowly to the door. Before he left, he turned around.

"We'll have to start early tomorrow morning. Very early," he said, and then left.

David was alone in the studio for the first time. He looked round again. There was another picture at the end of the room. It was the one David had noticed before, and it still had a cover over it. It was the one that Sharp was doing alone; the one Sharp had never told David about. He went over to it and lifted the dust-cover. He stepped back in surprise. It was a painting of a young woman with green eyes. She was wearing a ring on one of her fingers. The stone in the ring was the same colour as the woman's eyes.

It was Jan de Groot's *The Lady With Green Eyes.* At least, it looked exactly the same. It was one of the most famous paintings in the world and the original was in the British National Art Gallery in London. He stared at it.

Then he noticed something else. The eyes. He had seen those eyes before. They were exactly the same shape and colour as Karen's. The face was different, but not the eyes. He put the cover over the painting again, turned off the light, and went out.

CHAPTER TWELVE

In the park

"I've never liked this place. It's a dangerous place to meet, very dangerous," Jenny said.

They were in the park. She spoke in a low voice. She was sitting on a bench with her back to David. The children and the dog were playing not far away.

"Is that why you didn't speak to me the other day?" David asked. When he spoke, he turned his head away. Nobody could see that he was speaking to her.

"I thought someone was following me," Jenny answered.

"Someone? Who?"

"It doesn't matter. I wasn't sure. I think I was wrong. But we can meet here only once more. We'll have to find a different place," she said.

David began to tell Jenny about the de Groot painting. As he did so, he felt terrible. He didn't really want to tell her anything about it at all. He didn't really know why.

"It sounds very strange. Why should Sharp forge a painting like that? It's far too famous a painting. He's always forged the work of second class painters before. Too many questions are asked about famous paintings," Jenny said.

David couldn't explain it either. And, as usual, he and Jenny had very little time to speak.

A few days later, on a Sunday, Karen suddenly turned to him at lunch. She had been away again.

"Don't you ever get tired of staying in this house, in this town all the time?" she said.

David was surprised. She had never spoken to him very much before. She seemed to want to talk to someone, and Sharp wasn't the right person. It wasn't easy to have a conversation with him. Even for Karen.

"Come for a drive in the country," she said.

They got into her sports car and drove off. The ground was white with snow but the sky was blue, very blue. She drove at very high speed.

"You seem to enjoy driving fast," he said.

"Afraid?"

"Aren't you?" he asked.

"Yes, but I enjoy that, too!"

After a while they stopped and had coffee in a restaurant. They could see the mountains in the distance.

"My father's beginning to like you," she suddenly said.

"He's a strange man. I don't think I quite understand him," David answered.

She stared at him over the coffee cup.

"But I understand him. I've taken care of him for a long time. Ever since my mother died. Ever since I was a little girl."

David wondered if she would say more. But she turned and looked at the heavy snow on the mountains.

"I wish I were up in those mountains now. I really feel free when I'm up there. The only other time I feel free is when I'm driving really fast."

She looked back at him and then said with great feeling,

"I wish I were a man! Women are never really free!"

"You mean they always have to take care of husbands or children... or fathers?" David said.

He stared at her for a moment and then went on.

"If you want to be free, why don't you leave your father? Why don't you lead a life of your own?"

She shook her head.

"I have a duty to my father."

"Why? Because he's your father?"

"No. Because he's a great man. And I'm the only one he has."

David was surprised when she said the words 'great man'.

"What sort of great man?"

"A great artist, and I have to help him," she answered.

David was even more surprised.

"Help him? To do what?"

"To prove that he's a great man, of course," she said.

"But how can you do that?" he asked.

She finished her coffee and stood up.

"The time will come," she answered.

He didn't understand at all, but she didn't explain. They got back into the car and drove towards Zurich.

Another week went by. David learned more and more of Sharp's most important secrets. For example, he learned the secret of Sharp's paints. They were new but they dried quickly. Soon they were as hard as paints that were 350 years old.

David learned that Sharp used two chemicals in the paints. They were phenol and formaldehyde. Paints with these chemicals got dry and hard very quickly. But there was still a problem. Phenol and formaldehyde were only 100 years old. Neither chemical had been in use 350 years ago.

"Couldn't an expert find these chemicals if he used chemical tests?" David asked Sharp one day. Sharp was showing him how to mix the paints. Sharp smiled at the question.

"Of course he could. That is, if he dug into the painting and took some paint from it. But that doesn't happen very often," he answered.

"Why not?"

Sharp smiled again. He pointed to a bottle of varnish. The varnish is the colourless oil that is put on after the paint is dry. It protects the paint. Sharp always used very thick varnish. And it was exactly like the varnish painters had used 350 years ago.

"The first thing an expert looks at is the varnish. And the frame. And all the things he can see on the outside. He doesn't dig into the painting. Not very often," he answered.

David still didn't understand.

"But... why not?"

"If he dug into it, he would make a hole in the painting. Only a small one, but still a hole. Would you want an expert to do that if you had paid a lot of money for a painting? I don't think so. Experts do that only with very important paintings. Even then, they don't like doing it."

David had another question. It was difficult to ask. Perhaps Sharp would get angry. The question was about Sharp himself. Karen had said her father was a great artist. And Sharp wanted to believe this, too.

"Don't you ever get tired of painting other men's ideas? Don't you ever want to do original things?" David asked suddenly. He watched Sharp carefully.

Sharp was painting. He suddenly put down his brush. David watched his face. Sharp didn't get angry; not at first.

"When I was a young man I did only original work. And I always signed my own name."

He began quietly. But now his face went dark a little. His voice rose a bit with anger.

"Do you know what happened? They laughed at me!" he said.

"Who do you mean by 'they'?" David asked.

"The critics, of course. And all those owners of art galleries! I wanted to paint the human face and the human body. I wanted to show these things clearly... and simply. I wanted everybody to understand my paintings. I wasn't interested in all this modern art... cubes and squares and shapes that only the artist himself can understand."

He stopped again, and then said with great feeling:

"Art should be something for all people, not just for critics and rich people... and other artists. It's the painter's duty to make things as easy to understand as possible."

He was getting very excited. He stopped and then went on more quietly.

"I went to America. My wife came with me. I taught in an art school but then the art school closed. I tried to live from my paintings but nobody wanted them. My wife was ill. It was winter in New York. In America doctors cost money. I didn't have enough even for food and heat." The dark look came over his face again. David had seen it before.

"Things were very bad. One day I walked past a shop that sold old things, old furniture and so on. There was an old painting in the window. The owner didn't know how old but I could see it was Dutch and well over 300 years old. It was a very bad painting by a very bad artist but I bought it. I studied the paints very carefully. Then, somehow, I got all the paint off the canvas. I painted a new picture on the same canvas, in the same frame. It was in the style of another Dutch painter, a better one, who had lived at the same time."

He suddenly laughed.

"I took the painting to a gallery. I'd been there before but they hadn't been interested in my work. I told them the painting was seventeenth century and had belonged to my wife. They gave me 5,000 dollars for it."

He laughed again. As before, it wasn't a happy laugh.

"And your wife?" David asked quietly.

"She died that year. Perhaps, if I'd done it earlier, if I'd got some money for a good doctor and enough food and heat, she would have been all right."

David saw Jenny in the park the next day.

"From now on we'll meet near the lake," she said.

She began to tell him about the new place but he wasn't really listening. He turned to her. She was sitting with her back to him on the bench behind him.

"Have you got any photographs of Sharp's wife?" he asked.

"Not with me. And don't look at me when you talk!" she said. A few seconds went by.

"Why do you want a photograph of his wife?" she asked in a low voice.

"I... I just have an idea, that's all. It doesn't really matter."

They didn't talk for very long. He knew Jenny didn't like the park.

"This place is all wrong. We must think of another place," she said again before she left. David sat there for a few minutes longer. It wasn't a very nice day. The snow had disappeared, but the wind was still very cold. It began to rain a bit. The rain was like ice. He got up and left the park.

David didn't see the man in the car. It was parked just outside the park, on the other side of the street. The man had seen Jenny leave the park, too. He was short and he had small eyes. It was George. He watched David walk back towards Sharp's house. He watched every movement.

CHAPTER THIRTEEN
Harry and George

It was the morning after David had seen Jenny in the park. It was still dark when a sound woke David. It was a car. It was driving away. He looked at his watch. It was five o'clock. The sun hadn't come up yet.

Karen wasn't at breakfast. And Sharp seemed strange and distant. He didn't even answer when David said "Good Morning!" There was a strange, heavy silence in the house that morning.

After breakfast Sharp went into his workroom. David was just sitting down in his part of the studio. He looked up and saw Sharp staring at him. Then Sharp closed the door. It was the first time he had closed it in a very long time. David stared at it in surprise. He began to work in the strange silence.

A few hours later, after lunch, he heard another sound. It was someone coming through the front door of the house. David wondered who had opened it. Then the door to the studio opened. It was George. He didn't waste time on words.

"Orton wants to see you," he said.

David was so surprised that he didn't know what to say for a few seconds.

"What? Here? He's here in Zurich?" he finally asked.

"No. You're coming with me. To London. Today. The four o'clock plane. Get some things. You won't need much."

"What does he want to see me about?"

"Just hurry up!"

David looked at the door of Sharp's workroom. It was still closed. He went to his room and threw a clean shirt, a pair of pyjamas and a toothbrush into a small bag. Then he remembered something. He had a flight plan in the room. It showed the times of all the flights between Zurich and London. He looked at it. There was no four o'clock flight to London.

He also had a very small pocket knife. It wasn't very much but it was better than nothing. He carefully put it between the strap of his watch and his wrist. Nobody could see it. He had a jacket on. He went downstairs.

There was another surprise. Harry was in the car downstairs. He was waiting when David and George came out. Sharp hadn't come out of the studio to say goodbye. They got into the car and drove off. Harry was at the wheel. George sat in the back seat with David.

"Why does Orton want to see me?" David asked again.

"You'll find out," George said.

"But why does he want to see me so suddenly?"

"Because it's important, that's why!" George answered.

"What's important?"

"Orton will tell you himself."

It was still winter and it was already beginning to get dark. They drove very fast. David looked at the streets racing past them.

"I thought you said we were going to the airport," he said.

"That's right. To the airport," George answered.

"But we're going in the opposite direction."

"We're taking a private plane. We have to go to a small airport outside Zurich," George said.

They drove on for over an hour. The mountains lay in front of them. They were getting closer and closer to them, and it was getting darker and darker.

The time passed in almost complete silence. Only the noise of the powerful, fast engine and that of a few passing cars could be heard. When they got to the mountains, Harry turned off the main road. They drove through small villages. David could see families sitting down to dinner in their warm, comfortable houses. Outside, everything looked peaceful and quiet. But it was different inside that car that raced through the evening. David began to feel very afraid. He crossed his arms and sat back. He knew he would have to do something, and do it soon. It would have to be something that took Harry and George by surprise. He had noticed that George kept his hand in his coat pocket all the time. David had a good idea what was in that pocket.

He carefully put his right hand up the bottom part of his left sleeve. The small pocket knife was still there, under the watch strap. He opened the blade and then got it into his right hand. George couldn't see it. They were driving through a forest now. There were trees all around and it was very dark inside the car.

"Monti, Alessandro Monti," David said suddenly. George looked at him in surprise.

"Wasn't that his name?" David asked. George said nothing.

"You're taking me where you took him, aren't you?" David said.

George suddenly turned on David. He pressed something hard into his side. It was a gun.

"Just keep quiet. Just shut your mouth," he shouted.

"Why did you kill him?" David asked.

"Just shut up!" George shouted again. Then he went on:

"We know all about you. I saw you talking to that policewoman in the park. We know all about her, too!"

Then George stopped talking. They drove on along the narrow road.

CHAPTER FOURTEEN

Escape in the snow

It was a clear night. The moon came out and shone through the trees. They were near the mountains, and heavy white snow lay all around them. Harry stopped the car on the narrow road. There were a lot of trees there.

"Wait here. I'll see if it's the same place as before," he said to George, and got out of the car.

He walked into the trees. David could see him in the moonlight, against the bright white snow. He was looking around at the ground. It seemed he was trying to find a special place, a place perhaps where the ground was soft, where it was easy to dig. George never took his eyes off David. David could hear him breathing heavily. He was watching David in the same way a large cat watches a very small mouse. He had the gun out of his pocket and was pressing it into David's side. It was his right side and David had the pocket knife in his right hand.

Harry stopped looking around. It seemed he had found the right spot. There were no other cars on the road and it was very quiet. Harry's voice suddenly broke the silence. He shouted something and George looked up. Just at that moment David suddenly pressed the pocket knife into George's hand. The hand that was holding the gun.

The knife was very small but it cut deeply into George's hand. At the same moment David moved quickly to the side. George shouted. The pistol went off. The bullet tore through the air where David's head had been only a second before. David remembered those karate lessons in the club in

London. He hit George with the side of his hand just above the throat. There was very little space in the car and it wasn't easy to hit him there. George dropped the pistol and put his hand to his throat. David hit him again. Then, in the dark car, he found the pistol on the seat and fell back. He rolled out of the door and onto the cold snow on the ground. He got up and began to run.

He heard another shot. Something tore through the air just above his head. Harry was shooting at him. David threw himself to the ground again and looked back. George had rolled out of the car, too. He was still holding his throat with one hand.

David could see Harry running towards him. He looked back again. George had fallen down but had got up again. He was coming towards David, too. Harry had a gun. George didn't. David pointed the pistol in Harry's direction and shot at him. The thing jumped in his hand. The bullet went over Harry's head. The pistol was almost useless in his hands. He pointed it at Harry again. He could hear George coming towards him.

David was still on the ground. George was close, very close. David looked back towards Harry and then at George. He drew back his leg and kicked George very hard. This time he hit him just below the knee. George fell on top of David at the same time. David tried to get up. George had got him round the throat. David smashed the pistol down on his head. George screamed and his hand fell away.

David got up and ran towards the trees on the other side of the road. Another bullet from Harry's pistol smashed into the trees just above David's head. Snow fell down. David ran on through the snow and trees in the cold, bright moonlight. His breath rose in clouds behind him as he ran. He reached some bushes. Another bullet tore through the air near him. David fell behind the bushes. He stayed there, not making a sound.

For a few seconds David could hear only his own breathing and the blood pounding in his ears.

"Get him. Kill him!" he heard George say in a weak voice.

He was holding his head. His head was bleeding and so was his hand.

"He's got my pistol," George said.

"But he doesn't know how to use it," Harry answered. He helped George to get up. George fell down again and then got to his feet for a second time.

"Here, take this," Harry said.

Something shone in the moonlight. It was bright and cold and metal. It was a very long knife. The two men began to come towards David.

"He's in those trees somewhere," one of them said.

"This time, finish him. No talk. A shot in the head. Then we'll put him where the other one already is," the other answered.

David stayed very still. He felt a hard stone in the snow under one of his hands. He packed snow around it. The snow was hard and icy and the stone made it even harder. He knew he couldn't do very much with the pistol. But he had only one snowball and there were two men. The two men came towards him. They didn't know exactly where he was. They stayed close to the ground and used the trees as cover. They got closer.

Just at that moment, David heard another noise. It was a car or a lorry and it was still a long way away. But it was coming towards them down the long, narrow country road. David could see the lights. The two men stopped for a moment and looked towards the lights.

"Quick. Get him. Find him!" one of them shouted.

David knew he had to stop that lorry. It was his only chance. George was on one side of him and Harry on the other. Neither could see him yet. George came closer but was looking away from him. David aimed the snowball at him. George looked up just as he threw it. It hit him in the face with great force. There was a soft, breaking sound, like a bone smashing. George screamed again and fell down. There was blood all over his face. At that same moment Harry saw David and fired. A bullet tore through one of his sleeves.

David got down close to the ground and fired back. Again the bullet went hopelessly wide.

Harry looked towards the lights and sound of the lorry. David aimed the pistol at him with both hands, closed his eyes and fired. Again, the thing jumped about in his hand like a wild animal with a life of its own. But when he opened his eyes again he felt the bullet had gone much closer. Harry looked at him, at George lying on the ground with his hands over his face, and then at the lorry again. He turned and ran towards the car.

David ran after him. Suddenly Harry turned and fired. David felt something very hot hit him in the shoulder. He was knocked to the ground. He rolled over. His shoulder hurt him terribly, but he still had the pistol. Then he heard the car start. Harry had got into it. David crawled along the ground on his hands and knees. He aimed at the car. He had the pistol in both hands. He fired. Once. Twice. The car was already moving. He kept his eyes open this time and fired again. He knew there couldn't be many more bullets in the pistol. He fired once more. Suddenly the car seemed to shake. It went off the road and hit some trees. There was a terrible sound as the metal smashed against the wood.

Somehow David got to his feet and ran into the road. The lorry was coming towards him at full speed. David raised his arms and shouted. He stood there, alone in the centre of those bright lights as the lorry rushed towards him. The driver suddenly saw him and tried to stop. David could hear another sound. "The brakes," he thought. "The driver's putting on the brakes. But will he stop in time?"

He closed his eyes. He heard the lorry coming closer and closer. It was almost on top of him. He stood there and waited. He was sure the lorry would smash him to the ground. When he opened his eyes again, the lorry was only inches away. But it had stopped. The driver was staring at him, at the pistol in his hand, at the dark red blood all over his shoulder. The driver's mouth was hanging open. He got out of the lorry.

"The police. Get the police!" David said weakly.

The driver was still staring. His mouth was still hanging open in surprise.

"The police! Don't you understand? Get the police!" David said again. The driver came closer. Suddenly he pointed to the car. There was smoke coming from it. It was already beginning to burn. Together they ran to it and pulled Harry out. They carried him to where George was lying. There was blood all over George's face, where the hard, icy snowball had hit him. Harry looked terrible, too. There was a deep cut on his face. The lorry driver's mouth was still hanging open when he drove away to get the police. Harry opened his eyes. He couldn't understand what had happened.

David fell to the ground. He lay there and pointed the pistol at both of them. Harry began to move. He pushed himself up with one arm and stared at David. David pushed the pistol into his face.

"You!" David said. "Don't move. Don't do anything. Just stay there, or I'll..."

He pointed to the pistol. Then he pressed it even closer between Harry's eyes. David felt very weak but his voice was very loud. Harry fell back to the ground.

After the police had come, David looked at his pistol. There were no bullets left.

CHAPTER FIFTEEN

The body

The next morning the police began to dig up the ground. David thought he knew where the body was. He showed them.

"How do you know there's a body there?" the Swiss police inspector asked. They were near the spot where Harry had been.

"One of the men said something about it. I heard him. They were going to kill me and then bury me in the same place," David answered.

His shoulder was hurting him. A doctor had already taken care of it. Luckily, the bullet had passed through the top part of his shoulder. He felt very weak.

"I wonder why they wanted to use the same spot," David said.

"This is a good place to kill someone. Very few cars use the road at night. There aren't any houses. Nobody would hear the shot. And the ground is soft. Nobody would notice anything later. There aren't many places like it," the inspector said.

Just then, there was a strange sound. It was coming from somewhere above the trees. The sound came closer. David looked up and saw a police helicopter in the air. It looked like a very large metal insect. It hung in the air above the road for a few seconds, and then came straight down. A man got out. It was Moore.

"I caught the first plane to Zurich. Then I took a helicopter to get here as soon as possible," he said.

"What about Sharp? Have the Zurich police got him?"

David asked.

"I'll tell you more about that later," Moore answered.

David told him about the body. He pointed to the spot where the men were digging.

"I think you'll find Monti's body there," he said.

They watched the men digging for some time. Suddenly one of the men called out something. The Swiss inspector went over to the hole and looked down. The inspector called a policeman over and said something to him. The policeman got into a car and raced off in the direction of the village, a mile or two down the road. Then the inspector came over to David and Inspector Moore.

"Yes, Mr Rutland. You were right. There's a body there," he said.

The men dug again and then stopped. They got out of the hole. One of them looked back into it. It was clear that he didn't like what he saw. He suddenly held his hand to his mouth and ran behind a tree. David heard him making a strange, coughing noise. He turned away.

A few minutes later the police car came back. There was a police doctor inside. He got out, went over to the hole and then put some rubber gloves on. Then he got down into the hole. After a while he came out again and said something to the Swiss inspector. The inspector looked at David and Moore.

"A man. Young. Shot through the head. He's been dead about a year, the doctor thinks," he said.

"Monti disappeared about a year ago, didn't he?" David asked Moore. Moore nodded.

David suddenly felt sick again. He looked over at the hole.

"That was almost the way I ended. That was almost me," he said. Moore led him away to the helicopter.

"If you're well enough, there's still work for you to do. And it must be done quickly," he said. David didn't ask any questions. He was still thinking of that hole in the ground. The helicopter rose into the sky and flew off in the direction of Zurich.

The helicopter took them directly to the airport. During

the flight, David said nothing.

"And now about Sharp," Moore said after they had landed. David had forgotten about Sharp.

"Yes? What about him? Where is he now?" he asked.

"We don't know. He left his house late yesterday afternoon. He hasn't been seen since. And all the paintings have been taken away, too. They've disappeared."

David stared at him in surprise. Their flight to London was called over the loudspeakers.

"That's our plane. You've got to be in London as soon as possible," Moore said.

"Why?"

"Because Orton thinks you're dead. He doesn't know about George and Harry. Not yet. That's why I want you to go to his gallery."

David still didn't understand. They began to walk towards the plane.

"Go to his gallery? Me?" David said.

"Yes. And I'll be with you," Moore answered.

A few minutes later they were in the air, flying towards London.

CHAPTER SIXTEEN
In Orton's gallery

David and Inspector Moore went into Orton's gallery alone. Two policemen waited in the car outside. A young man came towards them. David had seen him before. It was the same young man who had spoken to him several months before.

"We'd like to see Mr Orton," David said.

The young man recognised him. He didn't smile carefully this time.

"He's very busy," he replied.

Moore showed the young man his police badge. He and David walked past him.

"You needn't show us the way. I already know it," David said. He led Moore up the balcony stairs.

David opened the door to Orton's office quietly. Moore was just behind him. Orton was dictating a letter into a tape recorder. He didn't hear the door open. David watched him for several seconds. He wondered what Orton would do when he saw him. He thought David was dead, lying in a hole in the Swiss mountains.

Orton suddenly looked up. His face went white. He stared.

"Have you heard from George or Harry yet?" David asked. He walked in. Moore followed him.

The cold look had gone out of Orton's eyes for once. There was a look of fear there.

"You!" he said. Then he noticed Moore behind David. His eyes moved from David to Moore and back to David again. A nerve moved in his face. He sat there. He did nothing. Slowly the cold look came back into his eyes.

"What are you doing here?" he demanded.

"I'd like to ask you a few questions," Moore suddenly said.

"Get out of my office at once or I'll call the police!" Orton shouted. He stood up angrily. Moore smiled and showed him his police badge. Orton sat down again.

"Do you know this man?" Moore asked and nodded towards David. Orton didn't even look in his direction.

"What are you talking about?" he said. His voice was nervous. He still hadn't got over his surprise.

"I think my question is clear enough," Moore said.

"No, I don't know him," Orton said coldly.

Moore smiled again.

"A moment ago you seemed to know him. You seemed very surprised at seeing him."

Orton paused. He spoke very carefully.

"Why are you asking me all these questions?" he demanded.

"Because we think you may be able to help us. Do you know him or don't you?"

"I meet a great many people every day!"

"Then how can you be sure you don't know him?" Moore asked quietly.

David stared at Moore. He couldn't understand why he was playing this cat and mouse game with Orton.

"I don't have to answer your questions. I shall say nothing more!" Orton said.

Moore gave him a card.

"I'd like you to be at my office at New Scotland Yard at three o'clock tomorrow afternoon."

Orton looked at the card.

"Is that an order?" he asked.

"Just be there, Mr Orton, that's all," Moore replied.

He nodded to David and turned to go. David followed him.

They walked down the stairs. When they got to the bottom, Moore stopped. The young man had already opened the door to the street for them.

"We'd like to see some paintings. You do sell them, don't you? Sixteenth century and seventeenth century originals?"

he said loudly. The young man's mouth fell open. He started to say something.

David was already looking around the walls. He soon found what he wanted. It was the drinking scene. It was one of the first pictures he had done with Sharp. He pointed to it and nodded. Moore turned to the young man.

"Have you a catalogue?" he asked.

The young man gave him one. Moore found the number of the painting in it and read aloud.

"Early seventeenth century Dutch original by Hans van Doorn."

He gave the catalogue back to the young man and said, "We shall need this painting for a few days. One of my men will come in to take it away. We'll take good care of it."

"What will happen now?" David asked after they had got into the car.

"We can't prove that Orton had anything to do with the murder of Monti. Not yet. That's why I want to see him tomorrow," Moore answered.

"But George and Harry work for him. And they killed Monti!" David said, almost angrily.

"We can't prove that either. And we still don't know if that was Monti's body. We'll have to wait. We'll have to see what George and Harry say to the Swiss police."

David fell silent. They drove past the National Art Gallery. David had told Moore about *The Lady With Green Eyes.* Neither he nor Moore knew where Sharp and Karen were.

"What if Sharp's in London now? What if he and his daughter try to steal the original painting?" David asked.

Moore shook his head.

"I don't think they'll try that. It would be impossible."

"Perhaps Orton has Sharp's copy," David said.

"Perhaps. But if he has, it isn't in Orton's gallery."

David didn't really think so, either. He remembered what Sharp had said to Karen. He had shouted that it had nothing to do with Orton. He sat back, wondering what was going to happen now.

CHAPTER SEVENTEEN

The two paintings

The old man was wearing dark glasses. He had a Swiss passport. It was forged, of course. He was staying at one of the best hotels in London. The passport said his name was Bruno Keppler. His daughter also had a Swiss passport. It was in the name of Karen Keppler.

They had just finished lunch in the hotel restaurant. Outside the sun was shining. There was a sign of spring in the air, but the wind was still cold.

"Nice day today," the waiter said.

The old man nodded.

"Going for a walk in the park?" the waiter asked.

"No. My daughter and I want to go to the National Art Gallery this afternoon," the old man answered.

David was in Moore's office. It was 2.30. He was looking through some photographs he had never seen before. The phone rang. Moore answered it.

"Yes. It was Monti's body," he said after he had put it down again. He went on: "That was a call from the Swiss police. George and Harry aren't saying anything. They refuse to talk."

David wasn't really listening. He was staring at one of the photographs. It was Sharp's wife. He had never seen one of her before.

At exactly 2.30 the old man and his daughter caught a taxi from the hotel. They looked like foreign tourists. The daughter was wearing a very long raincoat. They got into the back of the taxi. There was a glass window between them and the driver. He couldn't hear them talking.

"I've never done anything like this before. It's a big chance. All kinds of things could go wrong," she said.

"I know. I know. But I still want you to do it," he answered.

"The danger's far greater for you than for me. I'm sure I can get away. But can you, father?" she asked again.

The old man stared in front of him.

"I've told you before! That doesn't matter. Not any more."

He looked at his hands and then went on.

"The important thing is that people should know. They should see it with their own eyes. That's the only thing that's really important to me now. Perhaps I'm so old that I can't think clearly any more, but it's what I want." Then he turned to her.

"But you must leave the country as soon as it's over. Have you got your plane ticket and everything?" he asked.

She nodded, and said, "And there's one for you, too."

She showed him the two tickets. They were for a plane at 7.30 that evening to New York. He didn't really look at the tickets. They drove on to the gallery. When they went in, it was exactly 2.40.

In Moore's office David was still looking at the photograph of Sharp's wife. It wasn't a very good one, but there was still something very surprising about it. David had another photograph, too. It was from an art magazine; it was *The Lady With Green Eyes*. David's eyes moved from Sharp's wife and back to the famous painting.

"Look at this," he said quietly, but there was a note of excitement in his voice.

Moore came over and looked at the two pictures. At first he didn't notice anything.

"That's Sharp's wife. She died a long time ago," he said.

"I know it's Sharp's wife!" The note of excitement rose in

David's voice. Moore looked again. He suddenly took the two photographs from David's hands.

"Her face. It's... It's..." he began.

"It's the same as the woman in the painting! Exactly!" David finished the sentence for him.

Of course, the photograph of Sharp's wife wasn't in colour. But David already knew what colour eyes she had had. He had seen her daughter's eyes. And Karen's eyes were exactly the same colour as the woman in the famous painting.

"I've never noticed it before," Moore said, still looking at the two photographs.

"That's because you've never thought of looking!"

"Do you think it's possible that Sharp painted *The Lady With Green Eyes*?" Moore said.

David shook his head.

"I just don't know."

Moore walked up and down, thinking.

"We know that for the last twenty years Sharp has been doing forgeries of second class paintings. Never really great work."

David was thinking, too. He suddenly remembered some of the things Sharp had said.

"Perhaps Sharp has always hated himself for doing such work, for doing forgeries of paintings that were never great. His daughter once told me he was a great artist. Perhaps, when he was younger..." He didn't go on.

"But if he painted *The Lady With Green Eyes*, it wasn't really a forgery. Nobody has ever seen the original," Moore said.

David stared at him.

"But then why should he make another copy?" he asked. Moore shook his head. "And why should he want to steal the original?"

Moore looked at his watch. It was almost three o'clock. Orton would arrive at any minute.

"If that's what he really wants to do, it'll happen at night.

His daughter always works at night. I'll put a special police guard in the gallery after it closes."

At three o'clock Sharp and Karen went into the special room where *The Lady With Green Eyes* was on show. It was a small room at the end of a much larger one. The only way into the smaller room was through the larger one. Both were very crowded. The smaller room had two doors which were open. There was a guard just inside the doors. They walked past him and looked at the painting. Karen looked around the small room. There was another door there, but it was always closed. She knew it led to some workrooms. It was locked from the other side. They stayed there for a few minutes and then walked out again. Nobody in the crowd noticed them.

Orton arrived five minutes late. Moore began to question him immediately about Monti.

"Yes, I knew him. But so did a thousand other people. That doesn't prove anything, does it, Inspector?" Orton said.

Moore began to ask about the drinking scene he had found in his gallery.

"Perhaps it's a forgery. But I didn't know that when I bought it. And I paid a very high price for it," Orton said.

"And who did you buy it from?" Moore asked.

"From a collector here in England. I'm afraid I can't give you his name. He's very rich, and doesn't want his name in the newspapers. I'm sure you understand that, Inspector."

"So you're saying Sharp sold it to this collector, who then sold it to you?"

Orton smiled at Moore's question.

"I have no idea where he got it. But if you say so, I'm sure you must be right. After all, the police are never wrong, are they, Inspector?"

It was four o'clock. Karen and Sharp were in another part of the gallery.

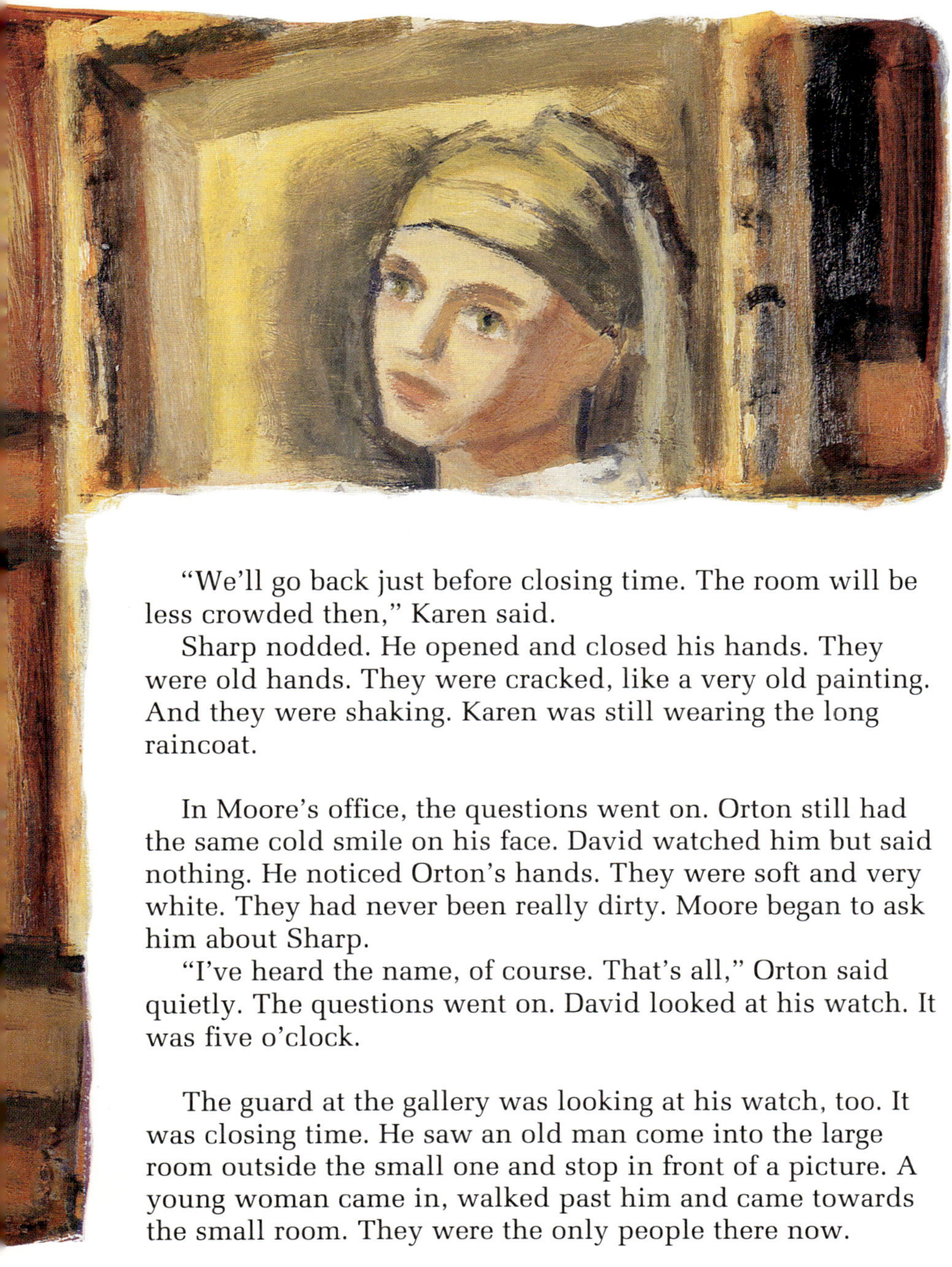

"We'll go back just before closing time. The room will be less crowded then," Karen said.

Sharp nodded. He opened and closed his hands. They were old hands. They were cracked, like a very old painting. And they were shaking. Karen was still wearing the long raincoat.

In Moore's office, the questions went on. Orton still had the same cold smile on his face. David watched him but said nothing. He noticed Orton's hands. They were soft and very white. They had never been really dirty. Moore began to ask him about Sharp.

"I've heard the name, of course. That's all," Orton said quietly. The questions went on. David looked at his watch. It was five o'clock.

The guard at the gallery was looking at his watch, too. It was closing time. He saw an old man come into the large room outside the small one and stop in front of a picture. A young woman came in, walked past him and came towards the small room. They were the only people there now.

The girl had stopped just outside the two doors leading to the small room. A bell began to ring in the gallery. The guard got up from his chair.

"We're closing now," he said.

The old man at the far end of the room looked at him and nodded. He turned to leave. Suddenly he put his hands to his head and fell to the floor. The guard stared at him. He walked towards him, past the young woman. His back was turned when she walked into the small room.

Karen worked quickly. She opened her long raincoat and took out a long steel bar from an inside pocket. Then she closed the two doors and pushed the bar between the handles. The guard heard them close but it was already too late. He ran towards the doors but there was nothing he could do. Inside the room, Karen also took out a small black thing. It looked like a bomb. She pulled a pin and smoke began to come from it. She threw it on the floor. With the same movement she took off the raincoat. A painting was sewn inside the coat. She tore it out. Only a few seconds had gone by. The smoke was getting thicker. There were pieces of tape on all four corners of the painting. It didn't take her long to hang the painting on the wall. Then she began to pound on the small door that led to the workroom.

"Fire! Fire!" she shouted. She pounded on the door again.

The guard in the large room outside was trying to get the two doors open, but the steel bar made it impossible. At the same moment an alarm bell began to ring in the gallery. The smoke was getting worse. It filled the small room. Karen shouted and pounded on the small door to the workroom. Someone opened it from the other side. It was a workman. There was another man with him.

"You can't come in here!" he shouted, and then stopped when he saw the thick black smoke.

"Fire! Can't you see? Do something!" Karen shouted. She ran past him into the workroom, shouting, "Fire!" The smoke from the small room came into the workroom. She ran out, down some stairs and then into the street outside. It was exactly 5.05.

CHAPTER EIGHTEEN
The arrest

Moore and David got to the gallery at 5.15.

There was still smoke in the large room and the small one, but the two doors leading to the smaller one were open now. They stared at the wall. *The Lady With Green Eyes* was still there. But there was another one there, too. It was on the wall next to it. The second painting was not in a frame, but it was the same in every way as the first. There was only one difference. The name on the first was 'Jan de Groot'. The name on the second was very very clear. It was 'Bruno Sharp'.

"But why? Why should he want to do this?" David said.

"He'll tell you himself. He's in an office downstairs. He tried to get away but we stopped him. I almost think he wanted to be caught," one of the guards said.

Sharp was sitting in a chair. He was staring in front of him. Two policemen were there, too. But Sharp didn't seem to notice them. He was far away in his thoughts. He looked up when Moore came in. David was behind him.

"I've been hoping to meet you for a long time," Moore said.

Sharp didn't seem to hear him at first. He stared.

"Which newspaper do you write for?" he asked.

He looked past him. He still hadn't noticed David.

"And where are the other reporters? The photographers? Where are they?"

Moore didn't answer at first. He noticed the far-away stare

in Sharp's eyes.

"Is that why you did it? So that all the newspapers would write about you?" he asked Sharp quietly.

"The whole world should know. You must tell them," Sharp answered.

"Tell them what?" Moore asked.

Sharp stared at Moore. He was beginning to get excited. "Everyone thinks I'm a forger, that I have no ideas of my own. They think *The Lady With Green Eyes* is Jan de Groot's work. They say it's great. A great original idea. A great, original painting. Well, that idea, that painting, is mine."

He was breathing heavily. He had to stop.

"I'm a policeman, not a reporter," Moore said quietly.

But Sharp wasn't really listening. He went on.

"For the last twenty years I've had to forge expensive but second rate pictures. Rich people bought them to show they were rich."

He looked at Moore.

"Can you understand how terrible that is for a man like me?" He pointed to his head.

"Up here there have always been original ideas. But nobody has wanted them. But once I painted one of those ideas. And I put the name of a great artist on it. Remember! Nobody had ever seen the original of *The Lady With Green Eyes*. There were just a few words in a book. I took those words and made them into a great painting. But nobody knows it's my work!"

Moore stood up. He looked at David and then back at Sharp.

"Orton says you've never had an original idea in your life!" he suddenly said.

David found it difficult to hide his surprise. Orton had said he didn't even know Sharp. Moore was watching Sharp carefully. There was silence again in the room. Complete silence. Sharp was breathing very heavily.

"Orton knows! Orton has always known!" he said.

He began to get very angry.

"Orton was in New York when I painted the original. I

can prove that. My wife was the model for the painting. I can prove that, too. Orton was working in a small art gallery there at the time. After I had finished the painting, there was a problem. I had to get it to Europe. It had to be found there. Orton helped me. We sent the painting in the bottom of a case to Holland."

"A case? What kind of case?" Moore asked.

"A case of coffee. My wife's family imported it. Orton had a friend in Holland. They say he killed that friend later."

"And the friend was the man who found the painting in Holland?"

Sharp nodded.

"That was the story. People had to think the painting had been in a house in Amsterdam for hundreds of years. Orton's friend had an aunt there who had just died."

Moore asked Sharp why Orton had killed the other man.

"Money. I got half the money. Orton and his friend got the other half. But I don't know anything about that side of things. I worked for Orton later. He got very rich. But I never had anything to do with that side of things!"

"What about Monti? Alessandro Monti? What about him?" Moore asked.

"That was something between Orton and Monti. I had nothing to do with that side of things!" Sharp said again.

Sharp was getting weak. David saw he couldn't go on much longer. But Moore didn't stop.

"But Monti worked for you, Mr Sharp!"

Sharp buried his head in his hands.

"Monti wanted more money for his own work. I don't know what happened. I think he said he would tell the papers about Orton and me if Orton didn't give him more. I had nothing to do with that side of things. Nothing," he repeated in a weak voice. Sharp was taken away. Moore was standing at the window, looking out.

"Why did you lie about Orton? He never said those things," David asked. Moore didn't turn around.

"The world is full of liars. Sometimes you have to tell lies to catch liars," he said softly.

CHAPTER NINETEEN
Karen

The whole story came out later. But it wasn't over yet. Sharp had done a lot of work for Orton. He told the police all about it. Orton had sold thousands of forgeries. Some of them were Sharp's. Others had been done by other artists, like Monti. Once an artist began to work for Orton, it was difficult to stop. Harry and George took care of that.

But some experts still said that Sharp hadn't painted the original *The Lady With Green Eyes*. They found small differences between the two paintings. Chemical tests showed that Sharp had used some modern materials in the copy. But the first painting had none of these. David showed them the photograph of Sharp's wife. Even this didn't really help. The experts still shook their heads.

"The photograph proves only one thing. Sharp's wife looked something like the model of the original painting. That's all."

Perhaps they wouldn't have said this if they had seen Karen Sharp's eyes. But Karen had disappeared.

Later, in prison, Sharp painted another picture in the style of de Groot. Like the first one, it was a picture that had disappeared. A Dutchman had written something about it in a book long ago. Experts watched Sharp paint the picture. He proved that even the most modern chemical tests weren't always enough. When it was finished, it was almost impossible to prove it wasn't over 350 years old. But the experts couldn't even agree about this.

One day David went to visit Sharp in prison. He was much weaker now and much greyer, but he smiled at David.

"You know I'm not lying. You must tell other people about me. You must tell them that I had ideas of my own," he said.

They talked for some time. Just before David left, Sharp said, "Perhaps some day you'll see Karen again. You must tell her that she did the right thing."

David didn't understand at first. Sharp went on.

"You see, she never wanted to leave me like that. She thought I'd be able to get out of the gallery. She thought I could get out through the front door. Everybody was leaving. It was closing time. But you know, I didn't really want to."

David never saw Sharp again. He died a few days later.

As usual, the experts couldn't agree. Even today some say Sharp really painted *The Lady With Green Eyes* and others say he didn't. David himself went to the United States and South America and talked to large groups of people about Sharp. He said he thought Sharp was far more than just a forger. But even he wasn't really sure. Could a real artist, a man with original ideas, paint other men's ideas for such a long time? And there were still a lot of questions he couldn't find answers to. Perhaps only Karen knew some of them.

But one thing was clear. Eric Orton was a man who had stopped at nothing. For him, art was only a good way to make money. He had even killed people. Orton, George and Harry were sent to prison for a very long time.

For David, the story never really ended. He couldn't forget Karen. Where was she? What had happened to her the day she ran out of the British National Art Gallery? He almost found out.

He was in New York one day. He had decided to take the underground railway, or 'subway' as the Americans call it. He was on a crowded platform. There was a young woman in front of him. He noticed her long blonde hair but he couldn't see her face. And then there was something about the way she moved. The train arrived and the crowd pushed forward. The train was already very full.

Half the people on the platform couldn't get in. The young woman leaped forward with a movement like a ballet dancer or gymnast. She turned around just as the door closed. David was outside. He looked up and suddenly saw the girl's face. She had green eyes. It was the first thing he noticed. It was Karen. He was sure of it.

He shouted her name and pounded on the glass window between them. For a moment the woman's face was frozen. She stared back at him. The eyes were cold. But then she smiled. She raised her hand and waved.

"Karen!" David shouted again and pounded on the window another time.

The train began to move. It gathered speed and disappeared into the tunnel.

READING ACTIVITIES

Before reading

1 The following art galleries are famous for their collections of European 'great masters'. Match the galleries with the correct city.

The Prado	London
The Uffizi	Paris
The National Gallery	Madrid
The Metropolitan	Florence
The Louvre	New York

2 Make a list of 'great masters' together with their nationality if possible. Compare your list with another person's.

3 This story is about a painter who makes money by forging or copying the work of other artists. What other things do people copy to make money? Think of three examples.

While reading

1 Who are the following people? Write *one* sentence about each of them.

a) David b) Karen c) Eric Orton d) Bruno Sharp e) Jenny

2 Which character says the following sentences and to whom? The answers are in Chapters 1–7.

a) "Someone came to help you last year. Do you remember?"
b) "If you want to sell the paintings, leave them here."
c) "And by the way, we'd pay you. We'd pay you on time."
d) "He isn't paid to talk. He's paid to do other things."
e) "I can do more than copy other people's work!"

3 After David leaves Scotland Yard in Chapter 3, imagine he telephones the young film director who owes him money. Write a short dialogue and act it out with a friend.

4 In Chapter 7, Karen shows Sharp a newspaper article about how the National Gallery bought *The Lady with Green Eyes.* Write this newspaper story, describing how the painting was found in Amsterdam ten years before. Give your story a title.

5 "But it's impossible, father!"

In Chapter 10, David overhears part of a discussion between Karen and her father. What do you think Sharp has asked Karen to do? Why does she say it's impossible? Write a possible dialogue leading up to Karen's reply.

6 Imagine that David keeps a diary while he is staying with Bruno Sharp. Record his entries for:

a) the day he arrives b) the day he goes into Sharp's studio c) the day of his first meeting with Jenny in the park.

After reading

1 Write out the summary, putting *one* word only in each gap.

Bruno Sharp and Eric Orton had ..... each other in New York. Orton was working in a small ..... gallery when Sharp ..... *The Lady With Green Eyes.* The ..... for this painting was Sharp's ..... . Sharp and Orton ..... the painting to Holland in the bottom of a ..... . Orton had a ..... in Amsterdam whose ..... had just ..... . They put the ..... in the dead woman's ..... . Everybody ..... the painting was the ..... of a ..... Dutch artist called Jan de Groot. It was ..... by a ..... in Amsterdam. Two ..... later, the man who had 'found' the painting ..... . His ..... was found in a ..... in Amsterdam.

2 Match the correct halves of the following sentences together:

a) After Jenny contacted David	Karen taped the painting to the wall.
b) After the police found Monti's body	Karen took off her black cap.
c) After David had had lunch	he was followed in the street.
d) After reaching her sports car	David and the Inspector left by helicopter.
e) After George saw David talking to Jenny	they began meeting in the park.
f) After she had released a smoke device	George and Harry came to Sharp's home.
g) After Orton offered David work	Sharp made him do some painting exercises.

3 Imagine you are the taxi driver who takes Sharp and Karen to the National Gallery in Chapter 17. Later that day you are interviewed by the police. Give your impressions of Sharp and Karen and describe how you picked them up.

4 Design a 'Missing' poster which the police issue in the hope of finding Karen Sharp. Include information about her appearance and age, what she was last wearing, where she was last seen, the reason she is wanted and who to contact with any information.

5 A few days after the story ends, imagine that David sees Karen again in the same subway station. This time he manages to talk to her and she tells him what has happened to her since her disappearance in London. How do you think their conversation ends? Write a short dialogue.

Material devised by Anne Collins and Jean Greenwood